The Lord's Prayer

Matthew 6:5–14; Luke 11:1–4 for children

Robert Baden
Illustrated by Kathy Mitter

CONCORDIA PUBLISHING HOUSE · SAINT LOUIS

The twelve disciples watched their Lord
As He knelt in prayer one day;
Then one of them approached and said,
"Lord, teach *us* how to pray."

So Jesus smiled and told His friends,
"Remember when you pray
You're talking to a loving God
And say your prayer this way:

"Dear Father, high on heaven's throne,
Great King of everything,
We come as Your dear children now;
Please hear the prayer we bring.

Father who art in heaven,

"As boys and girls come eagerly
To a mom or dad who cares,
We know that You are waiting, too,
To hear Your children's prayers.

"We know that You're the holy God,
But help us every day
To show the world Your holiness
In all we do or say.

"We know Your kingdom has no end,
But give us faith to share
Your love with all, so everyone
Can join us in this prayer.

Thy will be done on

"We know Your mighty will takes place
Without our words of prayer,
But we are weak and can't survive
Without Your watchful care.

earth as it is in heaven.

"Don't let the treasures of the world
Make us lose sight of You;
Please let Your Word show clearly what
Your will would have us do.

Give us this day our

"When we are hungry, give us food;
When tired, send us rest.
We know You'll give us all we need,
And it will be the best.

daily bread;

"And help us also realize
How You have blessed our days;
Help us appreciate Your gifts
And give You thanks and praise.

and forgive us our trespasses as we

"And when we fail to do Your will
And choose instead to sin,
Forgive us, Father. Call us back;
And make us Yours again.

forgive those who trespass against us;

"When evil things are done to us
And angry feelings start;
Teach us to be like You and speak
Forgiveness from the heart.

"When Satan comes with tempting words,
Help us to turn away;
Without Your power on our side
Sin always gets its way.

but deliver us from

"And when at last the hour comes
That death is standing by,
Come quickly then and take us home
To live with You on high.

"In heaven, above this world of pain,
Unhappiness, and tears,
We'll sing Your praise together with
The saints through endless years.

For Thine is the kingdom and the

GOD IS LOVE

"Dear Father, mighty King of all,
You rule with perfect love
In both Your kingdom of this world
And in the world above.

"All pow'r on heaven and earth is Yours,
And, yet, both great and small
Know that You'll hear and answer, too,
The prayers of one and all.

ower and the glory forever and ever.

"All glory is forever Yours;
You are the Holy One;
But also, Father, now accept
Our praise for all You've done.

"Now as we end our prayer to You,
We speak a loud 'Amen!'
We know You hear our words today
And seek our prayers again."

*O*ur Father who art in heaven,
hallowed be Thy name,
Thy kingdom come,
Thy will be done
on earth as it is in heaven.
Give us this day our daily bread;
and forgive us our trespasses
as we forgive those
who trespass against us;
and lead us not into temptation,
but deliver us from evil.
For Thine is the kingdom
and the power and the glory
forever and ever. Amen.